MONUMENTAL MILESTONES
GREAT EVENTS OF MODERN TIMES

Overview of the Persian Gulf War, 1990

A troop-carrying helicopter hovers over a carrier deck as elements of the U.S. fleet in the Persian Gulf steam toward Kuwait.

Mitchell Lane
PUBLISHERS

P.O. Box 196
Hockessin, Delaware 19707

Titles in the Series

MONUMENTAL MILESTONES
GREAT EVENTS OF MODERN TIMES

Overview of the Persian Gulf War, 1990

Key U.S. leaders during the Persian Gulf War: Secretary of Defense Dick Cheney (left), Chairman of the Joint Chiefs of Staff General Colin L. Powell, and commander of coalition forces General H. Norman Schwarzkopf.

Earle Rice Jr.

Mitchell Lane
PUBLISHERS

Copyright © 2009 by Mitchell Lane Publishers, Inc. All rights reserved. No part of this book may be reproduced without written permission from the publisher. Printed and bound in the United States of America.

Printing   1   2   3   4   5   6   7   8   9

Library of Congress Cataloging-in-Publication Data
Rice, Earle.
  Overview of the Persian Gulf War, 1990 / by Earle Rice Jr.
      p. cm. — (Monumental milestones)
  Includes bibliographical references and index.
  ISBN 978-1-58415-696-3 (library bound)
  1. Persian Gulf War, 1991—Juvenile literature. I. Title.
  DS79.723.R525 2008
  956.7044'2—dc22
                                                                    2008020932

ABOUT THE AUTHOR: Earle Rice Jr. is a former senior design engineer and technical writer in the aerospace, electronic-defense, and nuclear industries. He has devoted full time to his writing since 1993 and is the author of more than fifty published books, including *A Brief Political and Geographic History of Latin America: Where Are Gran Colombia, La Plata, and Dutch Guiana?*; *Blitzkrieg! Hitler's Lightning War; The Life and Times of Erik the Red;* and *Overview of the Korean War* for Mitchell Lane Publishers. Earle is listed in *Who's Who in America* and is a member of the Society of Children's Book Writers and Illustrators; the League of World War I Aviation Historians; the Air Force Association; and the Disabled American Veterans.

PUBLISHER'S NOTE: This story is based on the author's extensive research, which he believes to be accurate. Documentation of such research is contained on page 46.

The internet sites referenced herein were active as of the publication date. Due to the fleeting nature of some web sites, we cannot guarantee they will all be active when you are reading this book.

PLB

Contents

Overview of the Persian Gulf War, 1990

Earle Rice Jr.

*For Your Information

Iraqi tanks rumble along a broad boulevard leading into Kuwait City during Iraq's invasion of Kuwait on August 2, 1990.

Saddam Hussein, Iraq's despotic president-dictator, sent 100,000 troops pouring into tiny Kuwait on August 2, 1990. He falsely claimed that Kuwait was illegally taking oil from an Iraqi field. His unprovoked aggression drew the wrath of a multinational coalition and led to the Persian Gulf War of 1991.

Kuwait: Invasion and the Roots of War

Two hours after midnight on August 2, 1990, one hundred thousand of Iraqi dictator Saddam Hussein's crack troops rumbled across Iraq's southern border into tiny Kuwait. They streaked southward toward the Kuwaiti capital of Kuwait City in tanks, personnel carriers, and ordinary buses. The invaders consisted chiefly of three Iraqi Republican Guard divisions—two armored and one mechanized. They represented about one-tenth of Iraq's standing army, the largest in the Middle East.

Opposing them, Kuwait's tiny army numbered fewer than 16,000 troops. Against Iraq's mechanized might, the Kuwaitis could field only 250 tanks, 450 personnel carriers, and fewer than 100 artillery pieces. Their air force consisted of only 30 to 40 strike aircraft, two transports, and not a single bomber. The results of the ensuing clash were predictable.

At 2:00 A.M., in the Dasman Palace in Kuwait City, Jaber al-Ahmed al-Sabah, emir (leader) of Kuwait, awoke to the whine of jet engines and the whop-whopping of rotor blades. Saddam's warplanes and helicopter gunships were attacking strategic targets in the capital. The emir sprang up and rushed to his personal helicopter. It took to the air amid the developing chaos and whisked him to safety in Saudi Arabia. Moments after he left, an Iraqi chopper spewed a torrent of rockets into his vacated palace.

At the same time, troop-carrying Iraqi helicopters landed two Republican Guard battalions in the city. The elite troops began attacking strategic points around the capital. Within the hour, armored units of the Guard thundered into the city and joined the battle. Moving swiftly, they occupied key government buildings, communications facilities, and the central bank. Simultaneously, seaborne forces stormed ashore south of the capital and cut off the coastal road to Saudi Arabia.

Throughout the rest of the night, Radio Kuwait broadcast desperate appeals for outside help. The city's tiny garrison of soldiers—with help from the local police—fought valiantly against impossible odds. But by day's end, Kuwait City had fallen. And by noon the next day, all of Kuwait belonged to Saddam Hussein.

~

Iraq's invasion of Kuwait surprised most of the world but was not entirely unexpected. In mid-July 1990, some 30,000 Iraqi troops had deployed along the Iraq-Kuwait border. Their presence was an expression of Saddam's discontent. In February of that year, the Iraqi dictator-president had admitted that Iraq faced economic collapse. An eight-year war with Iran (1980–1988) had shoved his country to the brink of bankruptcy. The war had produced no clear victor, but the cost of waging it had left Iraq in debt to the tune of some $80 billion. Iraqi debts included more than $15 billion owed to Kuwait and another $25 billion to other Gulf nations.

To add to Saddam's woes, soldiers leaving Iraq's one-million-man army after the Iran-Iraq War found few jobs to return to in civilian life. The cost of maintaining such a large army in 1990 alone drove Iraq's military budget up to $12.9 billion. Saddam did not have that kind of money, but he had to do something. He borrowed more money and fell even deeper into debt.

Further, the rising inflation rate in Iraq stood at about 40 percent. Taxes already took about 72 percent of an Iraqi wage earner's annual income of roughly $1,950. Another increase in taxes would surely risk a civil uprising. Saddam knew he had to look outside Iraq to resolve his ever-growing money problems, and he looked first to the other Arab states in the Gulf region.

In February 1990, Saddam met with fellow members of the Arab Cooperation Council in Amman, Jordan. He all but commanded the Gulf states to bail him out of his financial difficulties. In addition to calling for an immediate freeze on his existing loan payments, he asked for a new loan of $30 billion to jump-start Iraq's economy. "Let the Gulf states know," he warned, "that if they [do] not give this money to me, I [will] know how to get it."[1]

Saddam followed his veiled threat with more audacious requests for financial help at the end of June. From each Arab member of the Organization of the Petroleum Exporting Countries (OPEC), he demanded $10 billion in aid. (OPEC is an international group of oil-producing nations. It was organized in 1960 to coordinate the petroleum policies of its member nations. OPEC attempts to control the price of oil by regulating oil production by means of a quota system. Each member nation is allowed to produce a set amount of oil over a given period of time.) To justify his demands, Saddam portrayed himself as the champion of Arab interests against the non-Arab Iranian revolution. Iraq, he pointed out, had sacrificed more men in the war with Iran than the other Arab states combined in their wars against Israel. In the Iraqi dictator's view, the Arab states all owed him for services rendered.

The other Arab leaders did not share Saddam's vision. Neither did they recognize how desperate the Iraqi dictator was to save his failing regime and fractured nation. Egyptian President Hosni Mubarak and Saudi leaders in the House of Saud pretty much ignored Saddam's pleas and threats. They declined to forgive his old debts or to favor him with new grants. An increasingly desperate Saddam turned next to his southern neighbor.

When the emir of Kuwait similarly rejected Saddam's pleas, Saddam accused Kuwait of stealing oil from the Rumaila oil field. The field lies mostly in southeastern Iraq but extends across the border into Kuwait. It ranks among the world's richest oil reserves. In the late 1930s, Iraqi leaders began to claim ownership of not only the Rumaila oil field but also Kuwait itself. Iraq's claim traces back to the old Ottoman Empire (c.1300–1899) when Kuwait formed a part of a *vilayet* (district) governed from Iraq. Saddam claimed Kuwait as Iraq's "nineteenth province." He also claimed rightful ownership of Warbah and Bubiyan, two desolate islands at the mouth of the estuary leading to Iraq's southern port of Umm Qasr. In any case, Saddam demanded $2.4 billion from Kuwait in payment for the "stolen" oil. Kuwait ignored him.

Saddam countered by again lashing out at the Arab oil-producing states. The United Arab Emirates and Kuwait bore the brunt of his anger. He argued that they were exceeding the production quotas set by OPEC and thereby shaving the price of oil. Their excesses, he claimed, were costing Iraq $1 billion a year in lost oil profits. Kuwait, on the other hand, figured that any profits derived from exceeding its oil quota were justified, and were just another way of recovering some of its war loans from Iraq.

On July 18, Saddam issued an ultimatum to Kuwait. It called for a stabilization of oil prices, a freeze on Iraq's wartime loans, and assistance in rebuilding Iraq. If the Kuwaitis refused to oblige, he warned, "We will have no choice but to resort to effective action to put things right and ensure the restitution of our rights."[2] Nine days later, Kuwait agreed to cut back on production to drive the price of oil up to $18 a barrel. The next day, however, Kuwait announced that its oil-production cutback would last only until the fall. Saddam responded by sending 30,000 more troops toward Kuwait—and so the Iraqi troop buildup along Kuwait's northern frontier continued.

Middle East observers believe Saddam had probably decided to invade Kuwait before he issued his ultimatum of July 18. With his military forces moving southward, only one issue remained unresolved. Since the fracturing of the Soviet Union the year before, the United States represented the only world power strong enough to deter his designs on Kuwait. The United States had supported Iraq in its war with Iran, but U.S.-Iraqi relations had cooled over recent months. Saddam wanted to secure at least a tacit approval of his impending action from U.S. President George H. W. Bush in Washington, D.C. With that in mind, he summoned April Glaspie, the U.S. ambassador to Baghdad, to a meeting at the Presidential Palace on July 25.

At his meeting with Glaspie, Saddam criticized the United States for supporting "Kuwait's economic war against Iraq."[3] He pointed out that Americans should be grateful to Iraq for having contained the Iranian fundamentalists. On a graver note, he threatened the United States with terrorist acts if it did not cease its hostile policy toward Iraq. "If you use pressure, we will deploy pressure and force," he cautioned. "We cannot come all the way to the United States but individual Arabs may reach you."[4]

Ambassador Glaspie replied mildly. "We have no opinion on Arab-Arab conflicts, like your border conflicts with Kuwait,"[5] she said. Saddam took her moderate response as a green light for his planned invasion of Kuwait. The coming months would show that he had clearly gotten his signals crossed.

President-dictator Saddam Hussein ruled Iraq by fear and force for almost a quarter of a century. His given name, Saddam, means "one who confronts" in Arabic. Over his years of ruthless rule, he became equally well known as the "butcher of Baghdad."

Saddam Hussein al-Tikriti was born to a peasant family near Tikrit, Iraq, on April 28, 1937. Orphaned at a young age, he went to live with an uncle who raised him. At age 15, Saddam moved to Baghdad with his uncle and family. In Iraq's capital, he applied to the Baghdad Military Academy—Iraq's version of West Point—but failed the entrance examination. In 1957, he joined the Ba'th Party, a political party founded in Syria during the 1940s. Its motto states: "One Arab Nation with an Eternal Mission."[6] Saddam became an enforcer.

In 1959, Saddam took part in a Ba'thist attempt to kill Abd al-Karim Qassem, the Iraqi prime minister. Wounded in the failed assassination attempt, he escaped first to Syria and later to Egypt. During 1962–63, he

Saddam as a young member of the Ba'th Party

studied law at the University of Cairo. When the Ba'thists took power in 1963, he returned to Baghdad and studied law at the university there. Later that year, opponents overthrew the Ba'thist regime and imprisoned Saddam for two years. He escaped and with a small group of associates led the Ba'thists back to power in 1972. He became president in 1979. His goals as president were to supplant Egypt as leader of the Arab world and to become the dominant authority over the Persian Gulf.

To help achieve his lofty aims, Saddam launched an invasion of rival Iran's oil fields in 1980. His campaign bogged down and dragged on to a stalemate in 1988. Iraq's economy nearly collapsed under the weight of wartime expenses. When Arab neighbors refused to lend Saddam more money to help Iraq's recovery, he decided to help himself to Kuwait's rich oil fields. He thought the world—particularly the United States—would not interfere with his aggression. Saddam thought wrong.

Saddam after his capture in 2003

A smiling General H. Norman Schwarzko[...] troops to ensure their combat readi[...] buildup for the Persian Gulf War.

General H. Norman Schwarzkopf, popularly known as "Stormin' Norman," served as the commander of coalition forces during the Persian Gulf War. Previously, he had served with distinction during two tours of duty in Vietnam and had led the U.S. invasion of Grenada. In the Persian Gulf, he was the right man in the right place at the right time.

Desert Shield:
Countdown to Conflict

On the day Saddam invaded Kuwait, U.S. President George H. W. Bush was hosting a conference in Aspen, Colorado. Margaret Thatcher, the British prime minister, was among those present. She spent most of the day with the president and assured him of Britain's support. Thatcher insisted that Britain's response to Saddam must recognize that "aggressors must never be appeased."[1] In her typical plucky approach to crises, she cautioned the president. "Remember, George," she said, "this is no time to go wobbly."[2]

President Bush realized that Saddam had just seized 15 percent of the world's oil reserves. An Iraqi invasion of Saudi Arabia—or even the threat of one—would enable Saddam to influence or control more than half the world's oil supply. The president moved swiftly to counter Saddam's aggression. Within hours of the invasion, President Bush froze Iraqi and Kuwaiti assets and imposed a trade embargo on Iraq. He also ordered the aircraft carrier *Independence* to move from the Indian Ocean to the Persian Gulf.

On August 3, in a rare show of solidarity, the United States and the Soviet Union issued a joint statement condemning the Iraqi aggression. Two days later, President Bush stepped off his helicopter onto the White House lawn. A reporter asked him about the deepening crisis in Kuwait. "This will not stand," he answered. "This will not stand, this aggression against Kuwait."[3]

On August 6, the United Nations (UN) called for Iraq's immediate withdrawal from Kuwait. Voting 13–0 with 2 abstentions, the UN Security Council passed Resolution 661. It imposed a total economic and trade embargo on Iraq. In so doing, it cut off the flow of oil through Iraq's export pipelines across Saudi

Arabia and Turkey. The Arab League also condemned Saddam's military adventure.

That same day, President Bush sent U.S. Secretary of Defense Richard ("Dick") Cheney and a party of advisers to Saudi Arabia. They conferred with King Fahd about hosting an American defense force. At an August 7 meeting in the Saudi capital of Riyadh (ree-YAHD), one of the king's advisers suggested waiting until Saddam showed clearer signs of his intention to attack. "The Kuwaitis delayed asking for help, and they are now our guests," King Fahd replied. "We do not want to make the same mistake and become somebody else's guests."[4] He agreed to host a strong American military presence.

Once President Bush decided to use the military, General Colin Powell, chairman of the Joint Chiefs of Staff, called on him to deploy a massive expeditionary force. If war came, he wanted to win it and win it quickly. He later commented, "We have a toolbox that's full of lots of tools, and I brought them all to the party."[5] It later became known that Saddam had not intended to invade Saudi Arabia at the time, but the United States had no way of knowing that. On August 7, President Bush ordered 2,300 men of the 82nd Airborne Division's ready brigade to Saudi Arabia.

On August 8, in Baghdad, the Iraqi Revolutionary Command Council authorized the return of the "branch, Kuwait, to the root, Iraq."[6] Baghdad announced the annexation of Kuwait, the first annexation of a sovereign state since World War II. The United Nations immediately declared the annexation invalid.

In a televised address that same night, President Bush told the nation that the U.S. 82nd Airborne Division had begun to deploy to Saudi Arabia. "A line has been drawn in the sand,"[7] he said, to repulse any further Iraqi aggression. Upon hearing the president's announcement, an Arab ambassador at the UN said, "Now let us pray that we can control the winds."[8] As of August 7, Operation Desert Shield—the military buildup of defense forces in Saudi Arabia—had begun.

President Bush's powerful speech of August 8 listed four guiding principles that would underpin his policy over the next six months. They called for (1) the immediate and unconditional withdrawal of all Iraqi forces from Kuwait; (2) the restoration of the Kuwaiti government; (3) the continued U.S.

commitment to stability in the Persian Gulf; and (4) the protection of American lives in the region.

Once committed to these principles, President Bush worked the phones and Secretary of State James A. Baker III toured the globe to seek international support. They formed a coalition of 34 nations willing to join the United States in a stand against Iraq. The president's concerns about Arab reaction to the possible use of arms against another Arab nation quickly faded. On August 10, the Arab League voted 12–9 to send troops to Saudi Arabia.

That same day, Air Force war planner Colonel John A. Warden III met with General Schwarzkopf in Tampa, Florida. Warden outlined a proposed air campaign, code-named Instant Thunder. The air campaign would later become the first phase of Operation Desert Storm, the offensive phase of the Persian Gulf War.

General Schwarzkopf, nicknamed "Stormin' Norman," headed the U.S. Central Command (CENTCOM). It constituted one of a series of joint regional commands established in 1983. CENTCOM, with its headquarters in Tampa, held responsibility for the Middle East. As its commander, the general would soon take charge of the largest mechanized combat operation since 1945.

On August 15, in a speech to Pentagon employees, President Bush added a fifth dimension to the need to roll back the forces of Saddam. "Our jobs, our way of life, our own freedom and the freedom of friendly countries all around the world would suffer if control of the world's great oil reserves fell into the hands of Saddam Hussein."[9] A week later, the president authorized the call-up of Reserves on August 22. Three days later, the UN called for the interdiction (cutting off) of Iraqi shipping in the Gulf. The rapid deployment of coalition forces into Saudi Arabia swung into high gear.

Tense days prevailed for the first three weeks. By month's end, the rest of the 82nd Airborne Division had arrived in Saudi Arabia, along with the 101st Air Assault Division and the First Marine Expeditionary Force (1MEF). Squadrons of F-15 fighters flew in from the United States. Two naval groups formed around the carriers *Independence* and *Eisenhower*. With a combined 150 strike aircraft, they stood in offshore positions in the Gulf. Until then, Saddam's forces could have wiped out the gathering coalition. "We were scared to death . . . ," General Powell said later, "there was no way we could have stopped him."[10] As additional coalition forces arrived, the pressure eased and the buildup went on.

General Schwarzkopf arrived in Riyadh on August 29. He set up his headquarters for Desert Shield in the Saudi Ministry of Defense building downtown. While the coalition forces assembled, he publicly declared that his mission was purely for the defense of Saudi Arabia. But on September 18, he ordered Army planners to begin work on a ground campaign. Coupled with an air campaign, the ground campaign would form the operational plan for Desert Storm. Called OPLAN 1002-90, it consisted of four parts:

- Deep air strikes into Iraq to take out Saddam's command, control, and communications facilities; industrial targets; airfields; and radar installations.

The U.S. carrier *Eisenhower* churns through the deep-blue waters of the Persian Gulf.

During Operation Desert Shield, the build-up phase of the Persian Gulf War, two naval groups formed in the Gulf around the U.S. carriers Eisenhower and Independence.

- Air attacks to destroy antiaircraft guns, missile sites, and radar posts in occupied Kuwait.
- Aerial and artillery bombardment of Iraqi troops to greatly reduce their fighting capability.
- A massive ground campaign to overwhelm and defeat a weakened and demoralized Iraqi army.

Ultimately, thirty-five nations would participate in Desert Storm, either militarily or financially or both: Afghanistan, Argentina, Australia, Bahrain, Bangladesh, Belgium, Canada, Czechoslovakia, Denmark, Egypt, France, Germany, Greece, Hungary, Honduras, Italy, Kuwait, Morocco, The Netherlands, Niger, Norway, New Zealand, Oman, Pakistan, Poland, Portugal, Qatar, Saudi Arabia, Senegal, Spain, Syria, Turkey, the United Arab Emirates, the United Kingdom, and the United States. U.S. troops made up 76 percent of the 660,000 coalition troops in the Persian Gulf.

By late October 1990, the troop buildup in Saudi Arabia had reached 250,000. In defiance of the coalition buildup, Saddam increased his forces in Kuwait to a half million. On November 8, President Bush ordered the U.S. troop deployment doubled to give them "an adequate offensive military option."[11] Diplomats searched for a peaceful resolution to the Gulf crisis. Coalition forces prepared for war.

On November 29, the UN Security Council stepped up the pressure on Saddam and passed Resolution 678. Twelve of fifteen nations voted for it; Cuba and Yemen opposed it; China abstained. The resolution authorized the use of force if Iraq did not pull out of Kuwait. It established a deadline of midnight (eastern standard time), January 15, 1991.

The new year began under the shadow of impending conflict. On January 9, Secretary of State Baker met with Iraqi Foreign Minister Tariq Aziz in Geneva, Switzerland. He engaged in a last-ditch effort to head off a clash of arms. The meeting resolved nothing. Four days later, on January 13, UN Secretary General Javier Perez de Cuellar flew to Baghdad for a final attempt at averting war. He also failed. Saddam Hussein interpreted both eleventh-hour attempts to reach a peaceful accord as a lack of will on the part of the United States and its allies.

In a live-fire training exercise during Operation Desert Shield, a British soldier burrows into the Saudi sand to provide covering fire.

On January 6, 1991, soldiers of Company C, First Battalion, of the UK First Armoured Division's Staffordshire Regiment participated in a live-fire assault on a mock village as the coalition forces trained for combat.

On January 12, the U.S. Congress voted to allow U.S. forces to conduct offensive operations. When the UN deadline for Iraq's withdrawal from Kuwait arrived at midnight on January 15, 1991, a half million Iraqi troops held firm. The world waited to exhale. And the last hopes for peace in the Persian Gulf ticked away in a final countdown to conflict.

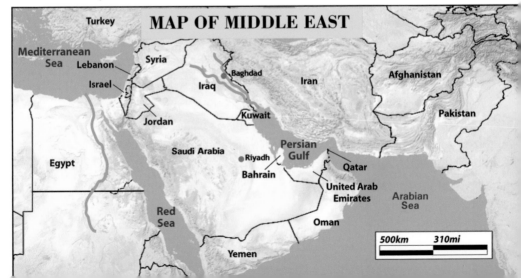

MAP OF MIDDLE EAST

Turkey

Mediterranean Sea

Lebanon

Syria

Israel

Baghdad

Iran

Afghanistan

Iraq

Jordan

Kuwait

Pakistan

Saudi Arabia

Persian Gulf

Egypt

Riyadh

Bahrain

Qatar

United Arab Emirates

Arabian Sea

Red Sea

Oman

500km   310mi

Yemen

FYInfo

FOR YOUR INFORMATION

George H. W. Bush, the forty-first president of the United States, knew war. As the pilot of a torpedo bomber in World War II, he flew many dangerous missions. On September 2, 1944, he was shot down during an attack on a Japanese-held island. He scored damaging hits on an enemy radio station before parachuting to safety. His two crew members did not survive. The U.S. submarine *Finback* rescued the future president from the ocean. The Navy awarded Bush the Distinguished Flying Cross for personal heroism during the incident. Forty-six years later, destiny called him to war again as his country's commander in chief.

George Bush as a navy pilot, 1942

Bush was born on June 12, 1924, in Milton, Massachusetts, a suburb of Boston. He attended exclusive private schools before enlisting in the Navy. After World War II, he entered Yale University; he graduated in 1948 with a degree in economics and was named to the Phi Beta Kappa honor society. He declined a position in his father's banking firm and set out for Texas, where he became independently wealthy in the oil business.

President Bush has Thanksgiving dinner with the troops during Operation Desert Shield

In the late 1950s, Bush became interested in politics. Over the next two decades, he served two terms in the U.S. House of Representatives, as U.S. ambassador to the UN, as head of the U.S. Liaison Office in China, and as head of the Central Intelligence Agency (CIA). From 1981 to 1989, he held the nation's second-highest office, serving as vice president to President Ronald W. Reagan. Bush reached the pinnacle of elective offices in 1988 when he defeated Michael S. Dukakis for the presidency.

Less than halfway into his term as president, Iraq invaded Kuwait. President Bush denounced the invasion and accused Iraqi dictator Saddam Hussein of an "outrageous and brutal act of aggression."[12] He drew a line in the sand in defense of Saudi Arabia, and he put together a coalition of nations to oust Iraqi forces from Kuwait. George H. W. Bush knew war.

A U.S. MH-53J Pave Low helicopter is [illuminated in the] ghostly green light of night photograph[y.]

During Operation Desert Storm, Pave Lows guided AH-64A Apache attack helicopters to enemy radar sites on the Iraq-Saudi Arabia frontier. The Pave Low can fly at night and in any kind of weather. Because of its advanced navigation and communications systems, it can fly as low as 100 feet and is used to conduct attack choppers into and out of enemy territory.

Desert Storm:
The Air Campaign

The January 15 deadline set by the United Nations for the withdrawal of Iraqi forces from Kuwait came and went, yet Saddam Hussein's troops remained in place. President Bush did not wait long to seek an alternative solution to the crisis on the Arabian Peninsula. His solution by force began with Operation Instant Thunder.

Just after midnight (local time) on January 17, 1991, two MH-53J Pave Low helicopters skimmed low over the Saudi desert toward the Iraqi frontier. The Pave Lows belonged to Air Force Special Operations and carried special navigation and sensing equipment. Their mission was to guide a flock of eight AH-64A Apache attack helicopters flying behind them to a pair of Iraqi air-defense early-warning radar sites near the Saudi border. The rocket-firing Apaches would then "neutralize" the radar sites, opening an air corridor to Baghdad.

The two radar sites stood some 35 miles apart. This unlikely flight of helicopters split off and arrived at their assigned targets at 2:30 A.M. "The destruction of these sites would blow a hole in Iraq's radar 'fence,'"[1] General Charles ("Chuck") Horner wrote later. Horner commanded the Ninth Air Force and CENTAF, the air component of CENTCOM. "When the time came," he continued, "the Apaches launched their Hellfire missiles, and moments later we had our fence hole."[2]

Hellfire missiles are air-to-ground missiles designed to be fired from attack helicopters. On this occasion, the Apaches destroyed 16 separate radar installations at each of the two sites. The deadly efficiency of the Hellfires opened up a 20-mile-wide air corridor straight into Baghdad. During the first seven hours of the Persian Gulf War, coalition aircraft flew more than 750 sorties into Iraq and Kuwait. (A sortie is one aircraft flying a single mission.) They delivered the most intensive aerial bombardment ever witnessed in the course of history up to that time.

Meanwhile, the U.S. battleship *Wisconsin* and the cruisers *Bunker Hill* and *San Jacinto* were firing off Tomahawk cruise missiles. The BGM-109 Tomahawk is a long-range, terrain-following missile for air, sea, and submarine launch. More than 100 Tomahawks were fired at Iraqi targets that night. The most unusual launches came from long-range B-52G bombers. They flew nonstop for more than 36 hours and a total of 14,000 miles from Barksdale Air Force Base in Louisiana. Their remarkable flight set the record for the longest continual air mission in history.

Bat-winged F-117A Nighthawk stealth fighter-bombers led the way into Baghdad. F-117As flew under the enemy's radar, undetected. They had to make their way through Iraqi air defenses and knock out systems radar, command

The U.S. battleship *Wisconsin* unleashes a salvo from its 16-inch naval guns off Iraq in 1991.

The Wisconsin *and her battle group arrived in the Persian Gulf on August 23, 1990. As part of Task Force Zulu,* Wisconsin *served as the Tomahawk Land Attack Missile (TLAM) strike commander. She contributed 22 missiles of her own and several dozen 16-inch shells to the assault on Iraq.*

bunkers, and communication sites—and they had to do it with no collateral damage. ("Collateral damage" is a term coined during the Vietnam War era to delicately define damaged, nontargeted—usually civilian—areas).

Close behind the Nighthawks flew a swarm of coalition aircraft from the United States, Great Britain, Saudi Arabia, and Kuwait. The warplanes represented an inventory of top-of-the-line combat aircraft. U.S. Air Force (USAF) pilots flew F-15E Eagles, F-111F Aardvarks, F-4G Wild Weasels (defense suppression aircraft), F-16A and F-16C Fighting Falcons, A-10A Warthogs, and B-52G Stratofortresses. Navy and Marine aviators piloted A-6E Intruders, F- and A-18 Hornets, A-7E Corsair IIs, and AV-8B British-made Harrier IIs. Army pilots in AH-64A Apache attack helicopters, according to one Pentagon official, "performed very well in a relatively limited role."[3]

About 150 Saudi F-15s, KC-135 Stratotankers, and E-3 AWACs (Airborne Warning and Control Systems) took part in the first strikes. Kuwaiti A-4KU Skyhawks also struck targets, as did Royal Air Force (RAF) Jaguars and Tornados.

Two hours into the opening air strikes, Saddam Hussein defiantly announced to the Iraqi people that "the mother of all battles had begun."[4] He had prepared his people for the coming storm. They were instructed how to protect themselves against chemical and nuclear attacks. Homes were blacked out. Medicine chests were stored in every home for emergency treatments. Iraqis had known hardship and deprivation during the long war with Iran, but few had experienced direct attacks on their homeland. This war would strike them where they lived.

Iraq had an extensive air-defense system and the world's sixth-largest air force, but its air defenses could not cope with U.S. radar-jamming and stealth technologies. Nor did the Iraqi air force challenge the overwhelming airpower of the coalition. Most of the few Iraqi planes that took to the air attempted to reach the safety of northern airfields.

The first attacks knocked out Iraqi command and control centers, radar sites, airfields, aircraft, and Scud missile sites. "Scud" is the term assigned by the North Atlantic Treaty Organization (NATO) to a series of tactical ballistic missiles developed by the Soviet Union during the cold war. All versions of the Scud derive from the German V-2 rocket of World War II.

Coalition attacks provoked only a limited response by the Iraqis. Defense Secretary Dick Cheney said, "It would be fair to say that we achieved a fairly high degree of tactical surprise."[5] Operation Instant Thunder boomed on for another five and a half weeks.

The Persian Gulf War became known as a "computer war" because it introduced so many new high-tech weapons. Cutting-edge weaponry included the Nighthawk stealth fighter-bomber that eluded radar and unleashed laser- and radar-guided "smart bombs." Cruise missiles, CBU-87 cluster bombs, BLU-82 "daisy cutters," and GBU-15 glide bombs added to the awesome array of munitions used in the conflict.

The Joint Surveillance and Target Attack Radar System (JSTARS) was also used for the first time in the Gulf. JSTARS consisted of 17 coded radio channels mounted in an E-8C aircraft (a modified Boeing 707). The highly computerized system directed satellite uplinks and a variety of radar systems. It provided early warning of enemy troop movements and targeted enemy forces for attack by deep-strike systems.

On January 18, Saddam Hussein answered the Allied air strikes by striking Israel with eight Scud missiles. He wanted to draw Israel into the war. By so doing, he hoped to cause the Arab members of the coalition to desert. The United States rushed Patriot missile-defense systems to Israel. Although not perfect, the Patriots added protection to Israelis under attack. Coalition aircraft hunted down and destroyed most of the fixed Scud launch sites. Scud launchers mounted on Soviet-made MAZ-543 launch vehicles proved hard to locate and troublesome throughout the war. Nevertheless, at the urging of the United States and others, Israel stayed out of the war.

Coalition aircraft continued round-the-clock air strikes. They destroyed four nuclear research reactors and severely damaged chemical and biological weapons facilities. Iraq's strategic and economic infrastructure shook under a constant pounding. Roads, bridges, power stations, and oil installations crumbled. By the end of January, much of Iraq lay in shambles. Saddam hoped to withstand the air attacks long enough to engage his enemies on the ground. "When the deaths and the dead mount on them," he predicted, "the infidels will leave."[6] But Iraqi morale reached a new low when about 100 Iraqi combat and transport aircraft flew to Iran to escape the war. Among troops along the Iraqi border, morale fell still lower under the carpet-bombing of B-52s.

During the Persian Gulf War, the United States deployed Patriot Antimissile and Antiaircraft Systems in the Gulf region to intercept Iraqi Scud missiles.

A U.S. MIM-104 Patriot missile leaves its launcher, possibly to intercept an incoming Iraqi Scud missile.

In a desperate effort to ignite the ground war ahead of the coalition timetable, Saddam set several Kuwaiti oil fields afire and began pumping crude oil into the northern Gulf. The seeping oil covered some 240 square miles and created the world's largest oil slick. Coalition ground forces did not budge. Saddam next launched a series of attacks on Allied positions.

On January 29, two Iraqi infantry and one tank battalion crossed the Saudi border and captured the deserted Saudi town of Khafji, about 12 miles to the south. Saudi troops, backed by U.S. Marines, quickly retook the town and drove the Iraqis back across the border. A few days later, four Iraqi mechanized divisions began massing near the Kuwaiti frontier town of Wafra. They approached in a ten-mile-long column with about 240 tanks and some 60,000 troops. Fierce coalition air strikes repeatedly ripped into the column and sent it reeling back in retreat. Saddam was forced to seek another solution to his worsening predicament.

U.S. Air Force attack aircraft—F-16A, F-15C, and F-15E—head north over burning Kuwaiti oil fields.

Although Saddam began destroying oil to bring the war to ground level, the coalition continued its air strike.

The Iraqi dictator had long threatened to use chemical and biological weapons if it became necessary. He did not. Many observers believe his restraint came from a behind-the-scenes warning of nuclear retaliation by the coalition. Instead of provoking his own demise with weapons of mass destruction (WMDs), Saddam turned to the Soviet Union for help in arranging a peace agreement. All Soviet efforts to broker a satisfactory peace arrangement failed when Saddam tried to impose conditions. He was in no position to dictate terms. President Bush gave Saddam until February 22 at 8:00 P.M. (local time) to unconditionally withdraw all his forces from Kuwait. Saddam did not.

On Sunday, February 24, President Bush announced that he had told General Schwarzkopf "to use all forces available to eject the Iraqi army from Kuwait."[7]

FYInfo
FOR YOUR INFORMATION

Star Performers

The Persian Gulf War erupted at 2:45 A.M. (local time) on January 17, 1991. On a moonless, starry night, coalition aircraft from the United States, Saudi Arabia, Kuwait, and Great Britain struck targets in Kuwait and deep inside Iraq. F-117A Nighthawk

stealth fighter-bombers and BGM-109 Tomahawk cruise missiles played leading roles in a drama of destruction. Slipping unhindered through Iraqi air defenses around Baghdad, they raised the curtain on a new era of computerized warfare.

The F-117A Nighthawks were the first of these high-tech performers to arrive at center stage over the Iraqi capital.

F-117A Nighthawk

Nighthawks are stealth-attack jet aircraft of triangular design, with flat, angled bodies. Wing panels direct radar reflections in a few specific directions. The panels aid the aircraft's radar-evading capability. The F-117s were designed in the 1980s as a highly classified "black project." They first saw combat action in Operation Just Cause, the invasion of Panama in 1989–90. During the Gulf War, F-117As flew 3 percent of the total missions (some 1,788 sorties), but they destroyed 43 percent of the total targets.

The BGM-109 Tomahawk is a long-range, all-weather cruise missile with stubby wings. It was designed by General Dynamics Corporation in the 1970s. Its original mission was to deliver nuclear warheads into the Soviet Union from aircraft and offshore ships. The Tomahawk Land Attack Missile (TLAM) comes in several operational versions. TLAM-Cs drop a 1,000-pound warhead on large, fixed targets. TLAM-Ds dispense bomblets (little bombs) against smaller targets in the field. Onboard computer systems guide the missiles to their targets. Cruise missiles flew 333 missions in Operation Desert Storm at a total cost of $380,300,000. Tomahawks tallied a success rate of almost 90 percent.

Playing off each other, Nighthawks and Tomahawks turned in star performances in their lethal roles over Iraq.

BGM-109 Tomahawk Missile Features

Booster

Conventional Land-Attack

Nuclear Land-Attack

Common Aft Section

Conventional Ship-Attack

Characteristics
Missile: **Common external shape, aerodynamics, and aft section**
Length: **20 feet**
Diameter: **21 inches**
Wing Span: **8 feet, 7 inches**
Propulsion: **Air-breathing Turbofan Engine; Solid Propellant Booster used for sea and ground launch**
Approximate range:
1300 nm—Nuclear Land-Attack
60 nm—Conventional Land-Attack
(nm=nautical miles)

A U.S. soldier directs the launch of an M-220 Tube-launched, Optically tracked, Wire-guided missile (TOW).

The United States uses the TOW—a crew portable, vehicle-mounted, heavy antiarmor weapon system—to engage and destroy enemy armored vehicles, primarily tanks. It is effective from ranges up to 4,101 yards (3,750 meters). After firing, the gunner must keep the crosshairs of the sight centered on the target to ensure a hit.

Desert Storm:
The Ground War

Coalition aircraft pounded Iraqi troops and strategic targets from the air for 38 days. By late February 1991, Iraqi troops had lost much of their will and ability to fight. The time for ground action had arrived. General Schwarzkopf called his plan for taking back Kuwait Operation Desert Sabre. He and his staff based it on the latest guidelines for "AirLand Battle," laid out in the U.S. Army's field manual *FM 100-5: Operations.*

Basically, the plan called for the penetration and encirclement of an enemy in two major thrusts: a frontal attack to fix the enemy in place, and a left-end sweep to cut off his avenue of retreat. This plan would force the enemy to surrender or face annihilation. World War II leader General George S. Patton described the tactic as "Hold 'em by the nose and kick 'em in the pants."[1]

For six months, coalition land forces had massed along a broad front from the Persian Gulf to Rafha on the Iraqi-Saudi border. The First Marine Expeditionary Force (1MEF) anchored the right (east) front, the XVIII Airborne Corps formed on the left (west) front, and the armored VII Corps assembled in the middle. General Schwarzkopf tabbed the Marines and an all-Arab corps to execute the frontal attack into Kuwait. For the left-end sweep, he named a mix of U.S., British, and French armored and airborne forces—VII Corps and XVIII Airborne Corps. VII Corps fielded four armored divisions, including one British. And XVIII Airborne Corps lent the weight of four more divisions, including the French Sixth Light Armored Division.

The objective of the frontal assault was Kuwait City and the vital road junction just to its left. While the Marine/Arab attack drew attention to southwestern Kuwait, the enveloping armored forces were to thrust around and through the elite Iraqi Republican Guard. Airborne forces to the far west would block Iraqi reinforcements heading south to Kuwait from Baghdad.

Operation Desert Sabre began at 4:00 A.M. (local time) on February 24, 1991. Marines of the First Marine Expeditionary Force (1MEF) attacked under the covering fire of 155-millimeter howitzers. Cobra helicopters and M-60 tanks led their advance in a chilling rain. Thousands of marines followed in armored personnel carriers (APCs) and high-mobility vehicles (HMVs, or Humvees). Iraqi artillery greeted their attack, but their big guns soon fell silent under the pounding of answering guns and close air-support attacks.

Marines of the First and Second Marine Divisions (part of 1MEF) worked their way through well-designed but poorly defended Iraqi berms and trenches with unexpected speed and ease. (Berms are mounds or walls of earth.) General Schwarzkopf later described the Marine advance as a "classic breaching" of enemy positions that would be "studied for years."[2] Throngs of surrendering Iraqis actually slowed the forward progress of the marines.

U.S. Marines advance into Kuwait at the start of the ground phase of the Persian Gulf War on February 24, 1991.

U.S. Marines of the First Marine Expeditionary Force (1MEF) spearheaded the assault on Kuwait during Operation Desert Sabre. By February 26, the marines had stormed to within ten miles of Kuwait City.

At 8:00 A.M., far to the west of the marines, 300 helicopters from the 101st Air Assault Division blasted their way into Iraq. In the largest wartime helicopter operation ever, they advanced about 120 kilometers (74.6 miles). Troops and supplies airlifted into Iraq established a forward refueling and supply base called the Cobra zone. This base sustained the 101st as the division pressed farther into Iraq to cut off enemy forces to the south and east.

In the meantime, the French Sixth Light Armored Division, with a brigade from the 82nd Airborne Division attached, angled north and west. The fast-moving French and Americans quickly overran an Iraqi air base at As Salman. From there, they protected the main force against a possible enemy thrust from the Baghdad area.

Throughout Desert Storm, U.S. special operations units teamed with British Special Air Service (SAS) and Special Boat Service (SBS) commandos in Kuwait and deep inside Iraq. They gathered critical intelligence information and provided rescue capability for downed pilots. These special-ops forces also helped track down mobile Scud launchers.

At noon, the Tiger Brigade of the U.S. Second Armored Division moved up and through the breach in the Iraqi lines cleared by the Marines. They drove a wedge between two Iraqi corps and broadened the lane to Kuwait City. On both sides of the Marines and Tiger Brigade, all-Arab units attacked north— Egyptian, Syrian, and Saudi troops in the west, and Saudi, Kuwaiti, and Gulf Arab forces along the coast in the east. (Gulf Arabs consisted of troops from Bahrain, Oman, Qatar, and the United Arab Emirates.) These all-Arab forces were officially called Joint Forces Command, North and East, respectively.

Also at noon, the balance of XVIII Airborne Corps began advancing in a long, northeastward arc. Led by the Third Armored Cavalry Regiment, and followed by the 24th Mechanized Infantry Division, they struck along a ten-kilometer (6.2-mile) front. They attacked toward the main Iraqi communication lines along the Euphrates (yu-FRAY-tees) River in tanks, armored vehicles, and helicopters. Against weak resistance, the Third Armored Cavalry covered 125 kilometers (77.7 miles) in 24 hours.

It soon became clear that the movement of coalition forces into Kuwait had succeeded in attracting the attention of Iraqi commanders. They responded by shifting reserve forces and some elements of Republican Guard southward. The shift exposed them to heavy air attack. Meanwhile, Iraqis in Kuwait City blew up the desalinization plant, the city's only source of drinking water. This signaled their intent to leave the city.

At this point, General Schwarzkopf decided to speed up his timetable. "If we moved fast," he wrote later, "we could force them to fight at a huge disadvantage; if we stayed with the original timetable, they might escape relatively intact."[3] At three o'clock that afternoon, General Schwarzkopf "let loose the main attack of Desert Storm."[4]

Spearheaded by the U.S. First Mechanized Infantry Division, with support from the British First Armored Division, VII Corps smashed through Iraqi defenses west of the Saudi-Kuwaiti frontier and pressed on. Farther west, the First and Third Armored Divisions attacked north, while the Second Armored Cavalry Regiment swung around the exposed Iraqi right flank. The entire corps moved in a northeast-to-east direction into Kuwait and Iraq. By nightfall, coalition forces had killed hundreds of Iraqis and captured more than 10,000 prisoners. Coalition casualties numbered 8 dead and 27 wounded.

Before dawn on February 25, the Fourth Marine Expeditionary Brigade aboard amphibious assault vessels in the Gulf feinted (faked) an invasion from the sea; Navy SEALs set off explosive charges along the beaches; and Naval Special Warfare teams linked up with Kuwaiti resistance fighters in Kuwait City. These diversions kept several Iraqi divisions tied up while coalition land forces drove hard toward their assigned objectives. While advancing through the burning Burgan oil field in Kuwait, the 1MEF and the Tiger Brigade engaged two Iraqi divisions in the largest tank battle in the history of the Marine Corps. Iraqi Soviet-built T-72 and T-62 tanks proved no match for U.S. M1A1 Abrams tanks. Marine and Army tanks destroyed 100 Iraqi armored vehicles. By day's end, coalition troops had shattered several Iraqi divisions and killed hundreds more Iraqi troops. The prisoner count rose to about 25,000.

On February 26, day three of the ground war, VII Corps began its eastward turn and tore straight into the elite Republican Guard. By then, the XVIII Airborne Corps had established blocking positions along the western front. Marines of the 1MEF, already within ten miles of Kuwait City, bore down on their objective of the Kuwait International Airport. Meanwhile, in Kuwait City, Iraqi troops began looting and stealing all available transportation for a massive retreat up a four-lane highway north of the city.

A Patriot Advanced Capability Radar "listens" for incoming enemy missiles.

Soldiers of the 24th Infantry Division's 72nd Engineering Company test a tank-mounted mine-clearing rake during Operation Desert Storm.

France's AMX-10RC wheeled armored reconnaissance vehicle, with a TK 105 turret with a light 105 millimeter gun, saw heavy service in the Gulf War.

A Soviet-built T-54 tank was disabled and left to rust as the Iraqis retreated north out of Kuwait City.

One of the fiercest battles of the war broke out when the Second Armored Cavalry Regiment (VII Corps) turned east to meet the Republican Guard. At a gridline on the regiment's map identified as 73 Easting, the Americans sliced through two crack Republican Guard divisions. In the ensuing Battle of 73 Easting, the Americans destroyed 29 Iraqi tanks and 24 armored personnel carriers, and captured 1,300 prisoners in less than half an hour.

By the end of the third day, Saudi forces had reached the outskirts of Kuwait City. U.S. forces had driven to positions in Iraq to the south of Nasiriya (nah-see-REE-yah). Many of their advances came despite blinding sandstorms, heavy rainfalls, an excess of mud, and the absence of air support because of deteriorating weather conditions. These advances virtually ended the war. Coalition forces had decimated more than 20 Iraqi divisions. The prisoner count was nearing 40,000.

That night, Baghdad radio reports announced to the world that all Iraqi forces would withdraw from Kuwait in accord with UN Resolution 660. "Everybody at headquarters felt very proud," General Schwarzkopf recalled later. "I was happy as hell."[5] News from the U.S. barracks at Dhahran (da-RAHN), Saudi Arabia, dampened their elation. A Scud missile had struck the barracks, killing 28 and wounding 100 men and women. It marked the largest number of U.S. casualties in the entire Desert Storm campaign. Some fighting remained to be done.

On February 26–27, elements of VII Corps broke the back of Saddam Hussein's vaunted Republican Guard in two great tank battles at Phase Line Norfolk and Medina Ridge. The rout was on.

The Iraqi Al-Hussein missile, a modified version of the Scud missile, has a range of 400 miles and can carry chemical or biological weapons.

Like 73 Easting, Phase Line Norfolk was only a line on a map, but it marked the scene of another great tank battle. Located right next to 73 Easting, some describe it as the second part of a two-part battle. The fighting at Norfolk started out badly for the Americans. Friendly fire killed six soldiers of the 41st Infantry Regiment (part of the First Infantry Division). Six American M1A1 main battle tanks and five Bradley Fighting Vehicles (BFVs) also fell victim to misdirected American fire.

Fighting began in earnest on the afternoon of February 26, 1991. The U.S. Second Armored Cavalry Regiment, Third and First Armored Divisions, and First Infantry Division (Mechanized) struck the Republican Guard Tawakalna Division at the Wadi al-Batin (a desert depression). Fierce fighting raged all afternoon and night. Red and green tracers arced across the sky. Cannon fire lit up the night a second at a time. Iraqi gunners destroyed two Bradleys. The Republican Guard fought bravely and well. In the end, U.S. tanks and technology pulverized the Tawakalna Division and left it broken beyond repair.

M1A1 Abrams tank

Farther to the north, early in the afternoon of February 27, the Second Brigade of the U.S. First Armored Division (VII Corps) collided with the Second Brigade of the Republican Guard Medina Division. The Iraqis had hastily dug defensive positions and shut down their tank engines. With cold engines, they hoped to elude U.S. thermal sights that locked on to heat. As soon as Iraqi tanks opened fire, however, U.S. Firefinder radar systems quickly located their positions despite their cold engines. American M1A1 Abrams tanks, 155-millimeter howitzers, and Apache attack helicopters took it from there. By midafternoon, American firepower had reduced more than 300 Iraqi tanks to smoking hulks of twisted steel. In the Battle of Medina Ridge, VII Corps effectively sealed off the last Iraqi escape route out of Kuwait.

AH-64A Apache helicopter

35

Americans gather to show support of U.S. troops returning from the Persian Gulf War.

After "no-win" wars in Korea and Vietnam—through no fault of those who fought in them— the quick, almost surgical performance of U.S. all-volunteer forces in the Persian Gulf War showcased the professionalism of a new breed of American Armed Forces.

Five Days and One Hundred Hours

Daybreak on February 27, 1991, found the French Sixth Light Armored Division and the Second Brigade of the U.S. 82nd Airborne Division positioned only 130 kilometers (80.8 miles) from Baghdad. By then, the 24th Mechanized Infantry Division had reached the Euphrates and wheeled to the right to launch a drive to Basra. It hoped to contain all Iraqi forces in a huge pocket south of the city. During its advance, the 24th shattered elements of two or three Republican Guard divisions and captured two Iraqi desert airfields. In four days, the division advanced 368 kilometers (228.7 miles). Its average daily movement of 92 kilometers (57.2 miles) ranks as the most notable advance in modern warfare.

To the right of the 24th Division, VII Corps continued to slug its way east toward Basra through a half dozen Iraqi divisions. In the center of a line running southeasterly, the First Cavalry Division and British, Syrian, and Egyptian forces decimated an entire Iraqi corps. They continued to press eastward to link up with the Marines. Meanwhile, the Marines prevented the Iraqis from retreating to the west.

At the same time, Kuwaiti, Saudi, and Gulf Arab forces entered Kuwait City from the south. Marines followed them into the city. They had backed off their rapid advance to allow the Arab forces to liberate the Arab city. Kuwaitis danced in the streets, waved Kuwaiti and American flags, and fired weapons in the air in celebrations resembling the Allied liberation of Paris in World War II.

A tightening ring of coalition forces left the Iraqis with no place to go but north. And north they fled, across barren deserts darkened by the caustic smoke of 250 burning Kuwaiti oil wells. Some 40,000 Iraqi troops streamed northward in loot-laden vehicles of every description.

"[R]eporters who had once been a part of media pools had taken pictures of Highway 6, where we'd bombed a convoy Monday night," General Schwarzkopf wrote later. "It was a scene of utter destruction that they named the 'Highway of Death.'"[1] The highway north, he continued, was "a four-lane road strewn with the burned-out wreckage of more than a thousand military vehicles and stolen civilian trucks, buses, and cars."[2] Air, artillery, and tank attacks by the Tiger Brigade all contributed to the destruction.

In Washington, President Bush grew concerned that folks around the world would view television coverage of the one-sided event as needless slaughter. Joint Chiefs of Staff Chairman General Colin Powell was already thinking of ways to end the war, and he asked Schwarzkopf what he wanted to do. The CENTCOM commander said that he needed one more day to completely destroy Iraq's military capability. He pointed out that the war by then would have lasted five days. "How does that sound to you: the 'Five-Day War?'"[3]

Chuckling, Powell replied, "That has a nice ring to it. I'll pass it along."[4]

By sundown on February 27, coalition forces had destroyed more than 33 Iraqi divisions. The prisoner count exceeded 50,000. A coalition victory appeared beyond all doubt. General Schwarzkopf held a press briefing in Riyadh. "The gate is closed,"[5] he said. Although Kuwait had not been completely sealed, he explained, Iraqi units could no longer retreat intact. "We've accomplished our mission," he said, "and when the decision-makers come to a decision that there should be a cease-fire, nobody will be happier than me."[6]

In Washington, President Bush conferred with his advisers about when to end the war. They finally decided to end it at midnight Washington time. White House Chief of Staff John Sununu pointed out that such timing would enable them to identify the ground campaign as the "Hundred Hours War." General Schwarzkopf later remarked about their decision with typical candor: "I had to hand it to them: they really knew how to package an historic event."[7]

On February 27, 1991, at 9:00 P.M. (eastern standard time), President Bush addressed a television audience and said, in part:

I am pleased to announce that at midnight tonight eastern standard time, exactly 100 hours since ground operations commenced and 6 weeks since the start of Desert Storm, all United States and coalition forces will suspend offensive combat operations. It is up to Iraq whether this suspension on the part of the coalition becomes a permanent cease-fire.[8]

Two hours after the president's television address, Iraq informed the United Nations that it had accepted all twelve resolutions issued by the Security Council against Iraq over the previous seven months. Iraq also had to agree to specific military conditions for a temporary cease-fire. Additional UN resolutions would later establish requirements for a permanent cessation of hostilities. One forceful condition insisted on the immediate release of all prisoners of war in Iraqi custody. For a while, more than a few people in the Arab world believed Saddam Hussein had won the war. Eventually, however, television footage changed the minds of most.

President Bush's announcement set the time of the cease-fire at 8:00 A.M. (local time) on February 28. During the hours between the announcement and the cease-fire, coalition forces continued to press ahead. The Iraqi Tenth Saladin Armored Division fought a desperate delaying action against marines and British and Arab troops advancing from the south. Many rated the Iraqi regular-army Saladins as Iraq's finest, but the great tide of coalition forces quickly swept them away.

To the west, VII Corps rolled on toward Basra to seal off the Iraqi escape route. Along the way, the First Armored Division continued to pound away at the Republican Guard. They severely crippled both the Medina and the Hammurabi Armored Divisions, two of the last effective Guard units.

At the appointed hour, the cease-fire took effect. Sporadic fighting continued here and there for several days, but the Persian Gulf War essentially ended at 8:00 A.M. on Thursday, February 28, 1991. The air campaign had pummeled the enemy for six weeks; the ground campaign finished the job in five days, precisely 100 hours after it had begun.

A community of nations of goodwill had banded together to deny the illegal aggressions of a tyrant against a helpless neighbor. President Bush summed

U.S. soldier Sergeant Quintan Hardy guards 112 Iraqi prisoners of war as the Persian Gulf War draws to an end.

U.S. M1A1 main battle tanks speed by a destroyed Iraqi tank after the liberation of Kuwait.

More than a thousand Iraqi military vehicles and stolen civilian vehicles were destroyed by coalition forces on the Highway of Death, a four-lane highway outside Kuwait City.

Gen. H. Norman Schwarzkopf (left) and Saudi Lt. Gen. Khalid Bin Sultan (center) sign the cease-fire agreement.

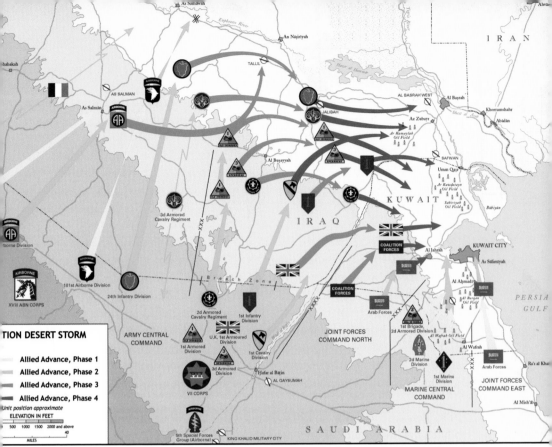

Operation Desert Sabre, the ground-war portion of Desert Storm, began on February 24, 1991. It took just five days for the coalition forces to advance from the Iraq–Saudi Arabia border to Kuwait City.

up the triumph: "This is a victory for the United Nations, for all mankind, for the rule of law, and for what is right."[9]

The U.S.-led coalition had achieved the aims set forth by President Bush in August 1990. It had ousted the Iraqis from Kuwait and restored the Kuwaiti government. Moreover, it had demonstrated a continued U.S. commitment to the stability of the region. And for the foreseeable future, Americans could safely conduct their affairs there.

On March 3, 1991, General Schwarzkopf met with his Iraqi counterpart, General Sultan Hashim Ahmed, at the southern Iraqi town of Safwan and negotiated Iraq's acceptance of the cease-fire terms. Flying back to Riyadh, the CENTCOM commander reflected on the past several months. He later wrote: "I looked down at the Kuwaiti sky still darkened with the stain of war, and at the unspoiled Saudi sky ahead, and told myself again and again, 'It is really over.' "[10]

Coalition forces achieved the original aims of President Bush and the United Nations in 43 days. They sustained surprisingly few losses. According to an official Pentagon tally, coalition personnel killed in action numbered 247. Of that number, 148 were American. Overall fatalities, counting noncombat deaths, totaled fewer than 500. The overall figure included 293 Americans. About a quarter of U.S. losses resulted from "friendly fire." Coalition equipment losses were also small, far less than expected. In the course of flying 109,876 sorties, the coalition lost only 38 aircraft (against more than 300 Iraqi losses).

Iraq suffered huge losses in Desert Storm. Coalition forces destroyed or seriously crippled 42 Iraqi divisions—almost one for every day of combat. In military terms, the divisions were rendered "combat ineffective." An estimated 25,000 Iraqi soldiers were killed and another 85,000 were captured. More than 100,000 troops simply deserted. Only about 15,000–20,000 troops remained in anything resembling combat readiness. Iraqi tank losses in combat reached 4,000. After the cease-fire, coalition forces destroyed captured and abandoned Iraqi military vehicles and equipment to prevent their future use. Cease-fire terms also enabled UN inspectors to destroy most of Iraq's remaining missiles, chemical weapons, and nuclear weapons facilities.

The Persian Gulf War of 1991 changed the face of modern warfare. It cast a new light on the importance of joint operations, lightning-fast air and armored operations, and precision-strike systems. Technology ushered in an age of all-weather warfare capabilities, complex electronic warfare and command and control systems, and the ability to strike deep behind the front lines. Desert Storm also demonstrated the growing influence of the mass media in shaping military procedures and operations. Largely because of television coverage, "collateral damage" became a household phrase.

Lastly, to a nation humbled by "no-win" outcomes to wars in Korea and Vietnam, Desert Storm showcased American fighting forces as the finest ever sent into combat. As for the despotic rule of Saddam Hussein, that would have to wait for another day.

Chapter Notes

Chapter 1   Kuwait: Invasion and the Roots of War

1. Con Coughlin, *Saddam: King of Terror* (New York: HarperCollins, 2002), p. 247.
2. Ibid., p. 249.
3. Ibid., p. 250.
4. Ibid.
5. Ibid.
6. Efraim Karsh and Inari Rautsi, *Saddam Hussein: A Political Biography* (New York: Grove Press, 2002), p. 13.

Chapter 2   Desert Shield: Countdown to Conflict

1. Con Coughlin, *Saddam: King of Terror* (New York: HarperCollins, 2002), p. 255.
2. Roger Hilsman, *George Bush vs. Saddam Hussein: Military Success! Political Failure?* (Novato, California: Presidio Press, 1992), p. 45.
3. Ibid., p. 46.
4. Thomas Houlahan, *Gulf War: The Complete History* (New London, New Hampshire: Schrenker Military Publishing, 1999), p. 13.
5. Ibid.
6. Coughlin, p. 257.
7. Hilsman, p. 47.
8. Ibid.
9. Ibid., p. 48.
10. Ibid., p.45.
11. Ibid., p. 88.
12. Coughlin, p. 256.

Chapter 3   Desert Storm: The Air Campaign

1. Tom Clancy, with General Chuck Horner (Ret.), *Every Man a Tiger* (New York: G. P. Putnam's Sons, 1999), p. 337.
2. Ibid.
3. Donald E. Fink, ed., *Persian Gulf War: Assessing the Victory* (New York: Aviation Week & Video Magazine, 1991), p. 148.
4. Con Coughlin, *Saddam: King of Terror* (New York: HarperCollins, 2002), pp. 263–64.
5. Fink, p. 148.
6. Coughlin, p. 268.
7. Ibid., p. 272.

Chapter 4   Desert Storm: The Ground War

1. Arthur H. Blair, *At War in the Gulf: A Chronology* (College Station, Texas: Texas A&M University Press, 1992), p. 109.
2. Andrew Leyden, *Gulf War Debriefing Book: An After Action Report* (Grants Pass, Oregon: Hellgate Press, 1997), p. 176.
3. H. Norman Schwarzkopf, with Peter Petre, *General H. Norman Schwarzkopf: The Autobiography: It Doesn't Take a Hero* (New York: Bantam Books, 1992), p. 453.
4. Ibid., p. 454.
5. Ibid., p. 467.

Chapter 5   Five Days and One Hundred Hours

1. H. Norman Schwarzkopf, with Peter Petre, *General H. Norman Schwarzkopf: The Autobiography: It Doesn't Take a Hero* (New York: Bantam Books, 1992), p. 468.
2. Ibid.
3. Ibid., p. 469.
4. Ibid.
5. Stephen Tanner, *The Wars of the Bushes: A Father and Son as Military Leaders* (Havertown, Pennsylvania: Casemate, 2004), p. 98.
6. Ibid.
7. Schwarzkopf, p. 470.
8. Andrew Leyden, *Gulf War Debriefing Book: An After Action Report* (Grants Pass, Oregon: Hellgate Press, 1997), p. 185.
9. Ibid.
10. Schwarzkopf, p. 491.

Chronology

August 2   Iraq invades Kuwait. U.S. President George H. W. Bush freezes Iraqi and Kuwaiti assets. United Nations (UN) calls for immediate Iraqi withdrawal from Kuwait.

August 3   United States and Soviet Union issue joint statement condemning Iraqi invasion.

August 6   U. S. Secretary of Defense Dick Cheney visits Saudi Arabia. Saudi King Fahd requests U.S. military assistance. UN Security Council passes Resolution 661 to impose trade embargo on Iraq, voting 13–0 with 2 abstentions.

August 7   Operation Desert Shield begins; United States starts to deploy military units to Saudi Arabia.

August 8   Iraq announces formal annexation of Kuwait. UN pronounces annexation invalid the next day.

August 10   Arab League votes 12–9 to send troops to Saudi Arabia. Colonel John Warden meets with General H. Norman Schwarzkopf in Tampa to outline air campaign.

August 22   President Bush authorizes call-up of Reserves.

August 25   UN authorizes military interdiction of Iraqi shipping.

September 18   General Schwarzkopf orders Army planners to begin work on ground campaign.

November 8   President Bush orders more troop deployments to give "an adequate military option" to U.S. forces.

November 29   UN Security Council passes Resolution 678, calling for use of force if Iraq does not withdraw from Kuwait by midnight (eastern standard time) January 15, 1991.

1991

January 9   U.S. Secretary of State James Baker meets with Iraqi Foreign Minister Tariq Aziz in Geneva, Switzerland, in a failed effort to find a peaceful solution to Kuwait crisis.

January 12   U.S. Congress votes to allow U.S. troops to conduct offensive operations.

January 15   UN deadline for Iraqi withdrawal from Kuwait reached.

January 17   Operation Desert Shield ends and Operation Desert Storm begins as coalition aircraft bomb targets in Iraq and Kuwait.

January 18   Iraq launches first Scud missile attack on Israel.

January 29   Iraqi forces seize Saudi port city of Khafji.

January 30   Buildup of U.S. forces in Gulf region exceeds 500,000.

January 31   Saudi and Qatari forces, backed by U.S. Marines, recapture Khafji.

February 22   President Bush issues ultimatum for Iraqi troops to withdraw from Kuwait.

February 24   Operation Desert Sabre (ground war) begins; U.S. Marines, Army, and Arab forces move into Kuwait and Iraq.

February 25   Iraqi Scud missile hits U.S. barracks in Saudi Arabia; 28 Americans are killed.

February 26   Iraqis flee Kuwait City.

February 27   President Bush orders a cease-fire, effective at midnight (local time).

February 28   Cease-fire takes effect at 8 A.M. (local time).

March 3   Iraqi military leaders accept cease-fire terms at Safwan, Iraq.

Timeline in History

1890	Idaho and Wyoming admitted to the Union.
1895	First professional football game played in the United States at Latrobe, Pennsylvania.
1898	U.S. declares war on Spain over Cuba.
1900	Quantum theory developed.
1905	Albert Einstein introduces the theory of relativity.
1908	General Motors Corporation formed.
1912	RMS *Titanic* sinks on maiden voyage after colliding with an iceberg; 1,503 drown.
1917	Allies execute Mata Hari as a spy.
1924	Mohandas (Mahatma) Gandhi fasts for 21 days to protest religious feuds between Hindus and Muslims in India.
1927	Charles A. Lindbergh flies monoplane *Spirit of St. Louis* nonstop from New York to Paris in 33.5 hours.
1931	Gangster Al ("Scarface") Capone convicted and jailed for income tax evasion.
1932	Lindbergh baby kidnapped.
1939	Adolf Hitler publishes *Mein Kampf* ("My Struggle").
1942	Italian-American physicist Enrico Fermi splits the atom.
1945	Rocky Graziano named Boxer of the Year.
1949	North Atlantic Treaty signed in Washington, D.C.
1954	J.R.R. Tolkien publishes *Lord of the Rings*.
1961	Exiled Cuban rebels unsuccessfully attempt an invasion of Cuba at the Bay of Pigs.
1963	President John F. Kennedy assassinated by Lee Harvey Oswald in Dallas, Texas, on November 22; Lyndon B. Johnson sworn in as president.
1968	North Koreans seize U.S. intelligence ship *Pueblo* on charge of violation of North Korean waters.
1970	Four student war protestors killed by the National Guard at Kent State University in Ohio.
1974	President Gerald Ford pardons former President Richard Nixon for any criminal offenses committed while in office.
1975	James R. Hoffa, former president of the International Brotherhood of Teamsters, vanishes.
1981	IBM introduces the personal or home computer.
1984	U.S. and French medical researchers independently discover the AIDS virus.
1985	British Antarctic Survey discovers a hole in the ozone layer over Antarctica.
1989	U.S. forces seize General Manuel Noriega for trial and conviction in the U.S. on charges of drug trafficking, racketeering, and money laundering.
1990	Germany celebrates the formal reunification of East Germany and West Germany.
1996	Dolly, a sheep created by cloning an adult cell, is born.
2001	Fundamentalist Islamic terrorists attack the World Trade Center in New York City and the Pentagon in Washington, D.C. Operation Enduring Freedom launches America's war against terrorism in Afghanistan.
2003	U.S. and coalition forces invade Iraq and depose Iraqi dictator Saddam Hussein in Operation Iraqi Freedom.
2008	Iraqi Prime Minister Nouri al-Maliki demands a timeline for the withdrawal of U.S. military forces.

Further Reading

For Young Adults

Carlisle, Rodney P. *Persian Gulf War.* New York: Facts on File, 2003.

Holden, Henry M. *The Persian Gulf War: A MyReportLinks.com Book.* Berkeley Heights, New Jersey: Enslow Publishers, 2003.

Nardo, Don. *The Persian Gulf War: The War Against Iraq.* Farmington Hills, Michigan: Lucent Books, 2000.

Santella, Andrew. *The Persian Gulf War.* Mankato, Minnesota: Compass Point Books, 2004.

Speakman, Jay R. *Weapons of War: The Persian Gulf.* Farmington Hills, Michigan: Lucent Books, 2000.

Works Consulted

Aburish, Saïd K. *Saddam Hussein: The Politics of Revenge.* London: Bloomsbury Publishing, 2000.

Blair, Arthur H. *At War in the Gulf: A Chronology.* College Station: Texas A&M University Press, 1992.

Clancy, Tom, with General Chuck Horner (Ret.). *Every Man a Tiger.* New York: G. P. Putnam's Sons, 1999.

Clancy, Tom, with General Fred Franks Jr. (Ret.). *Into the Storm: A Study in Command.* New York: G. P. Putnam's Sons, 1997.

Coughlin, Con. *Saddam: King of Terror.* New York: HarperCollins, 2002.

Darwish, Adel, and Gregory Alexander. *Unholy Babylon: The Secret History of Saddam's War.* New York: St. Martin's Press, 1991.

Dinackus, Thomas D. *Order of Battle: Allied Ground Forces of Operation Desert Storm.* Central Point, Oregon: Hellgate Press, 2000.

Fink, Donald E., ed. *Persian Gulf War: Assessing the Victory.* New York: Aviation Week & Video Magazine, 1991.

Giangreco, D. M. *Stealth Fighter Pilot.* Osceola, Wisconsin: Motorbooks International, 1993.

Hassan, Hamdi A. *The Iraqi Invasion of Kuwait: Religion, Identity and Otherness in the Analysis of War and Conflict.* Sterling, Virginia: Pluto Press, 1999.

Hilsman, Roger. *George Bush vs. Saddam Hussein: Military Success! Political Failure?* Novato, California: Presidio Press, 1992.

Houlahan, Thomas. *Gulf War: The Complete History.* New London, New Hampshire: Schrenker Military Publishing, 1999.

Karsh, Efraim, and Inari Rautsi. *Saddam Hussein: A Political Biography.* New York: Grove Press, 2002.

Khadduri, Majid, and Edmund Ghareeb. *War in the Gulf, 1990–91: The Iraq-Kuwait Conflict and Its Implications.* New York: Oxford University Press, 1997.

Leyden, Andrew. *Gulf War Debriefing Book: An After Action Report.* Grants Pass, Oregon: Hellgate Press, 1997.

Mackey, Sandra. *Reckoning: Iraq and the Legacy of Saddam Hussein.* New York: W. W. Norton, 2002.

Miller, John, and Aaron Kenedi, eds. *Inside Iraq: The History, the People, and the Modern Conflicts of the World's Least Understood Land.* Introduction by David Rose. New York: Marlowe & Company, 2002.

Morris, David J. *Storm on the Horizon: Khafji— The Battle that Changed the Course of the Gulf War.* New York: Free Press, 2004.

Munthe, Turi, ed. *The Saddam Hussein Reader: Selections from Leading Writers on Iraq.* New York: Thunder's Mouth Press, 2002.

Schwarzkopf, H. Norman, with Peter Petre. *General H. Norman Schwarzkopf: The Autobiography: It Doesn't Take a Hero.* New York: Bantam Books, 1992.

Sifry, Micah L., and Christopher Cerf, eds. *The Iraq War Reader: History, Documents, Opinions.* New York: Simon & Schuster, 2003.

On the Internet

Atkinson, Rick. *Fog of War,* "Murky Ending Clouds Desert Storm Legacy" http://www.washingtonpost.com/wp-srv/inatl/longterm/fogofwar/intro.htm

PBS: *Frontline: The Gulf War* http://www.pbs.org/wgbh/pages/frontline/gulf/

Schubert, Frank N., and Theresa L. Kraus, eds. *The Whirlwind War* http://www.history.army.mil/books/www/Wwindx.htm

Glossary

A-4KU (Skyhawk)—A carrier-based, single-engine, turbojet attack aircraft.

A-6E (Intruder)—A carrier-based, twin-engine, long-range, all-weather aircraft designed for low-altitude attacks.

A-7E (Corsair II)—A carrier-based, single-engine, all-weather, light-attack aircraft.

A-10A (Warthog)—Slang for the Thunderbolt II, a twin-engine, subsonic, tactical fighter-bomber.

AGM-114 (Hellfire)—U.S. air-to-ground missile designed to be fired from attack helicopters.

AH-64A (Apache)—An attack helicopter designed to destroy tanks and to provide close ground support for troops.

APC—Armored personnel carrier.

AV-8B (Harrier II)—An all-purpose, single-engine fighter-bomber designed to provide quick-response support for U.S. Marine ground troops; capable of vertical or short takeoffs and landings.

AWACS—Airborne Warning and Control System.

B-52G (Stratofortress)—U.S. long-range heavy bomber.

BGM-109 (Tomahawk)—A versatile, long-range cruise missile with surface or air launching capability, carrying a conventional or nuclear warhead.

BLU-82—U.S. 15,000-pound bomb known as the "daisy cutter"; capable of vaporizing everything within several hundred yards of its explosion.

CBU-87—U.S. bomb that releases multiple projectiles upon impact; used against personnel and vehicles; a cluster bomb.

CENTAF— U.S. Central Command Air Forces; the air component of Central Command.

CENTCOM—U.S. Central Command; one of a series of joint regional commands established in 1983; responsible for the Middle East and parts of Africa and Central Asia.

E-3 (Sentry)—A surveillance aircraft used as part of AWACS.

F-4G (Wild Weasel)—A specially equipped jet fighter aircraft used to detect and destroy enemy radar and missile installations.

F-15E (Eagle)—A single-engine, two-seat air-superiority aircraft equipped with high-definition radar.

F-16A/C (Fighting Falcon)—A single-engine, single-seat jet fighter known for its high maneuverability.

F-111F (Aardvark)—A medium-range, swept-wing bomber capable of carrying a large quantity of explosives.

F-117A (Nighthawk)—Stealth fighter; a highly advanced fighter-bomber used primarily for deep-strike missions.

F/A-18 (Hornet)—A carrier-based, twin-engine attack aircraft.

Firefinder—U.S. radar system that tracks the trajectory of incoming rockets and artillery rounds backward to their source.

FM 100-5: Operations—U.S. Army field manual used to plan air/land operations for Desert Storm.

GBU-15—A precision-guided, modular glide bomb.

HMV (Humvee)—High-mobility vehicle; also called "Hummer."

Jaguar GR.1 (SEPECAT)—French-designed tactical support jet aircraft used by both France and the UK.

JSTARS—Joint Surveillance and Target Attack Radar System mounted in an E-8C aircraft (a modified Boeing 707).

KC-135 (Stratotanker)—A four-engine turbojet aerial tanker/transport plane.

M1A1 (Abrams)—U.S. main battle tank; A1 version introduced in 1985.

M60—U.S. main battle tank before the M1 Abrams was introduced in 1980; used by U.S. Marines in the Persian Gulf War.

MAZ-543—Soviet-built missile launcher used by Iraq to launch Scud missiles.

MH-53J (Pave Low)—A large, heavy-lift helicopter equipped with terrain-following and -avoidance radar for low-level penetration.

Scud—Tactical ballistic missile developed by the Soviet Union during the cold war and used by Iraq in the Persian Gulf War.

SEAL—U.S. Navy SEa, Air, and Land special operations service.

T-62—Soviet-built medium tank.

T-72—Soviet-designed main battle tank.

TLAM—Tomahawk Land Attack Missile; Tomahawk cruise missile (BGM-109).

Tornado—A twin-engine, two-seat supersonic strike aircraft built by Panavia for use by the UK, Germany, and Italy.

Index